THE KEY TO ART

THE KEY TO PAINTING

Juan-Ramón Triadó
Professor of Art History

Lerner Publications Company · Minneapolis

Copyright ©1988 Editorial Planeta, Spain

Copyright © 1990 English language, David Bateman Ltd.

This edition published 1990
by Lerner Publications Company
241 First Avenue North, Minneapolis, Minnesota 55401, USA

In association with David Bateman Ltd.
32-34 View Road, Glenfield, Auckland, New Zealand

LIBRARY OF CONGRESS CATALOGING-IN-PUBLICATION DATA

Triadó, Juan-Ramón.
  [Claves de la pintura. English]
  The key to painting/Juan-Ramón Triadó.
      p.   cm.—(The Key to art)
  Translation of: Las claves de la pintura.

  Includes index.
  Summary: Traces, through text and color plates, the history of
painting, from early cave paintings to those of the twentieth
century. Discusses the history of the artist's tools and the use of
technique, perspective, proportion, and compositon.
  ISBN 0-8225-2050-8 (lib. bdg.)
  ISBN 0-8225-2053-2 (pbk.)
  1. Composition (Art) 2. Painting—Technique. [1. Composition
(Art) 2. Painting—Technique. 3. Art appreciation.] I. Title.
II. Series.
ND1475.T7513   1990
750'.1—dc20   89-12233
                                                    CIP
                                                    AC

A David Bateman Book

Printed in Spain
Bound in USA by Muscle Bound Bindery

1 2 3 4 5 6 7 8 9 10 99 98 97 96 95 94 93 92 91 90

INTRODUCTION

Painting is the visual art form best known to most of us. If you ask anyone to name a few painters, sculptors, and architects, most of those listed will be painters. We know their names from the great collections in art galleries and museums. Very often, however, we appreciate the fame of the artist rather than the real beauty of the work. Paintings, more than other works of art, must be appreciated for their form, meaning, and content.

Some knowledge of composition theory helps those trying to understand and appreciate a painting. It also helps to understand the conditions, as well as the time and place, in which the painting was created.

AUL CÉZANNE. *The ard Players*. 1890-95. lusée d'Orsay, Paris, rance.
he basic value of **form**, or esign, is clear in this picure. Cézanne's paintings ck any extra decoration. hey keep closely to what e considered essential—a nse of geometry, or the rangement of parts. Yet, is works always give e viewer much to ink about.

Abstract art, where form and color are more important than the subject, has greatly increased our understanding of painting styles. A painting should not be judged by its subject, but by the balance it achieves

3

ANONYMOUS, ITALIAN.
The Martyrdom of Saint Andrew. **End of 17th century. Diocesan Museum, Lerida, Spain.** Though the name of the painter of this magnificent work is unknown, he or she was certainly a great artist. Here we can appreciate a painting without knowing its creator. We can value and analyze the work itself. A painter becomes a **master**—an artist whose work is a model or an ideal—when he or she creates a new form of expression and maintains an overall high standard for a period of time.

between form and content. Abstract art gets idea across through shape, as well as line and color.

Our appreciation for the arts is firmly rooted i our feelings. Our personal tastes usually cause us t like or to dislike a painting. However, enjoying picture intellectually gives us a richer and less-biase appreciation. Try to avoid being influenced by ideas o feelings associated with the subject of the painting.

Visual understanding of a painting must be based
n the idea that form has meaning. Many critics
mphasize this fact. They talk about the life of form,
e spirit and the content of significant form. These
eas are important to any work of art.

Throughout this book we shall see that form has
reat significance and how form can influence our
ppreciation of a painting. By the **composition**, or

BENOZZO GOZZOLI. *Procession of the Magi.* **1459. Medici-Ricardi Palace, Florence, Italy.** In contrast to Cézanne, Benozzo Gozzoli considered painting as something ornamental and expressive. He used many details—all richly shown. The painting includes lifelike portraits of members of a family named Medici, who commissioned the painting.

arrangement, an artist uses, he or she takes us into the subject and controls what we are to see. The impact of composition depends largely upon the artist's abilities. The way the artist paints the work will determine how people will interpret and appreciate it.

Painting becomes a new reality—with a language and an internal life of its own.

A viewer must actually *look* at a painting. This may
~em to be an unnecessary statement, but it needs to
~ stressed. Many people can recognize and classify a
~ainting, but often they spend too little time looking at
. To such viewers—even if they are art experts—a
~py would be just as good.

The basic knowledge of unchanging factors

JAN VERMEER VAN DELFT. *View of Delft.* **1658-60. The Hague, Mauritshuis, Netherlands.**

Landscape painting is not just the imitation of nature, but the creation of a new reality based on nature. Here we are shown not just the city of Delft, but rather the artist's personal view of that city. It is this personal element that attracts us. The painting has an appeal of its own and it has its own reality.

governing the appreciation of a painting have to learned. This book deals with the traditional techniqu of painting, as well as with more recently develop techniques. It also looks at tools and surfaces used artists, as well as the elements, such as techniques a composition, that make up a painting.

THE ARTIST'S TOOLS

The painter has three basic tools: a palette, a brush, and a palette knife.

Hundreds of years ago, shells or bowls were used to hold paints after they had been mixed. Later, the small wooden **palette**—a thin, oval or rectangular board with a hole for the thumb—was developed.

The **paintbrush** is used to apply paint to the canvas and to provide texture. There is a different brush for each different technique and medium, or material. Normally, round-ended brushes are used for outlining, for blending, and for covering small areas. Short-haired brushes are used to produce thick coats of paint. Long-haired brushes serve to spread the color. Flat brushes are very versatile. Used sideways, they are perfect for outlining. Most brushes are made from bristles and hairs from animals, such as hogs, calves, camels, squirrels, badgers, and sables.

The **palette knife** is very flexible and is usually made of steel. It can be made of bone, ivory, or hard rubber to avoid a chemical reaction that might occur between a steel knife and the paint. The palette knife is mainly used to mix colors and to spread both primer and paint on the surface. It also is sometimes used directly on the surface to create very expressive open forms with paint.

Hands, sponges, and cloths are all used for creating special effects and finishes and for spreading paint.

Artists generally use pencils, pen and ink, charcoal, and chalk for drawing. Great Renaissance painters used silver-pointed styli to work on paper that had already been colored and coated. Then they found

MARINUS REYMERSWAELE. *The Money Changer and his Wife.* 1539. Prado Museum, Madrid, Spain.

Small pictures were often painted on wooden panels during the Romanesque and Gothic periods. **Tempera** paint, generally made of egg yolk, water, and pigments, is applied to a surface and becomes permanent when it dries. During the Renaissance,

that drawings made with lead-tipped stilettos w[...] erasable and did not require advance preparation the paper.

Conté made the first pencil with a mixture of c[...] and black lead crayon. It is still known today as a Co[...] crayon. Felt-tipped and ballpoint pens are only oc[...] sionally used by artists.

The pen has progressed a long way from the ea[...] use of reeds to the metal pen points of today. Amo[...] feather pens, goose quills were the most flexible us[...] but swan, raven, and turkey feathers were also used[...]

Works of art are also done in crayon, charco[...] pastels, and wax pencil. Today, backgrounds and spec[...] effects are sometimes achieved by using an airbrush[...]

SUPPORTS USED

pera was used on both
od and canvas. Painting
wooden panels was
ndoned in southern
ope during the 17th
tury. However, in central
ope, artists established
m tradition of using
oden panels. Careful
paration of the panel
ws artists to use deli-
e, precise brushwork.

ONYMOUS. *Large
on with Straight Tail.*
**eolithic art from
Altamira Caves.
ntabria, Spain.**
ve walls were one of the
liest surfaces on which
mitive people drew and
nted. The magical char-
er of these paintings
es not impair their
istic richness. These
ists sought perfection in
ir art and constantly
ed to create beauty.

People have always felt the urge to express themselves—their feelings, their myths, and their beliefs—as well as to record their possessions, their homes, and the landscape in which they live. The walls of the caves in which prehistoric people lived became surfaces to be decorated with images of all these.

However, throughout the history of art, wood and,

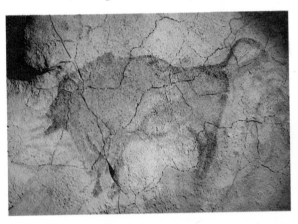

later, canvas, have been the most widely used supports for painting. Paintings on wood have been traced to ancient Egypt and Rome. In the Middle Ages, wood became more widely used, especially for religious frontals, polyptychs (hinged panels), and other altar pieces. Canvas gradually became the accepted surface for paintings during the Renaissance, although some artists still used wooden panels occasionally. Panels were made of white poplar, lime, willow, chestnut, cypress, fir, and mahogany woods. Today, fine, lami-nated three-, four-, or five-ply panels are often used. Some works are painted on canvas that is glued to

11

wood. This practice may combine the best of b[...] techniques.

Today, canvas is the most widely used mater[...] although linen, hemp, cotton, and jute fabrics are a[...] found. For small and medium-sized works, the b[...] material is pure linen. For larger surfaces, hemp[...] recommended. Canvas has to be primed before be[...] used. For a time, canvases were primed, or coat[...] with dark colors, but these gradually gave away[...] white or lighter colors. Other less commonly us[...] materials are silk, velvet, and satin.

The third most common support on which peo[...] have painted is walls. Murals from Minoan, Egypti[...] and Etruscan art and a few from Greek and Roman[...] have survived through the years. Mural painti[...] however, blossomed in the Romanesque peri[...] particularly during the late Gothic era and throu[...] out the Renaissance. During the Baroque period, wa[...] and ceilings were covered with highly decorati[...] images. The artist Goya used oil paint on canvas t[...] was glued to the wall to create his "black" paintings[...]

Much painting has also been done on copp[...] Seventeenth-century Flemish art contains good e[...] amples of small paintings with careful brushwo[...]

ÉDOUARD MANET.
Déjeuner sur l'Herbe.
1863. Musée d'Orsay, Paris.
Only during the Mannerist and Baroque periods did canvas really come into its own in southern European countries. Its light weight and ease of handling made it easy to transport and helped sales. Its lower cost and easy preparation were also important considerations.

ANONYMOUS. *Beatus of Cardeña.* **1200. Art Museum, Gerona, Spain.**
Vellum scrolls were frequently used by artists in the early Middle Ages. These were made from sheepskin or calfskin, carefully prepared to get a thin, translucent sheet of material. Scrolls were widely used for writing and illustrating the gospel story, Bibles, and missals from the 4th to the 13th centuries. Since many scrolls have been well preserved over the centuries, we are able to appreciate firsthand much Romanesque art that would have vanished if it had been painted on walls.

ANONYMOUS. *Christ of Saint Clement of Taüll.* **12th century. Museum of Catalan Art, Barcelona, Spain.**
Mural painting was at its finest during the Romanesque period. From murals on church walls, uneducated worshippers learned the Christian story. During the Renaissance, Michelangelo created his masterpiece on the ceiling of the Sistine Chapel in the Vatican, but in the Baroque period much of the storytelling part of mural painting vanished.

MANUEL TRAMULLES.
The Concert. **Second half of the 17th century. Museum of Modern Art, Barcelona.**

Since the 14th century, paper has been a popular surface on which to work out artistic ideas. As it became cheaper, paper allowed artists a freedom to experiment that was not available with other materials. It has been widely used, both for sketching and for finished works, because it is a versatile material that accepts charcoal, pencil, watercolor, and pastel with equal ease. Paper gives a work of art an immediacy and spontaneity not usually found elsewhere.

Zinc and tin have been used in the same way. Sl marble, and ivory are used, but rarely. Plastics and human body—either painted or tattooed—are ot supports on which people have drawn or painted.

Paper remains the ideal support for drawing. I especially prized for water-based painting when i made from linen because of its fine quality and ease with which brushes, sponges, or palette kni can be used on it. Cotton-based paper, if used watercolor or gouache, tends to absorb too much wa making the colors less vibrant and clear. Illumina manuscripts and pictures on scrolls were done by Greeks and the Romans, and such art flourishec the Middle Ages.

Cardboard, if properly prepared, can also be usec a surface for painting, but it is more often used drawing and sketching.

Paper is usually white, although indigo and paper was used during the Renaissance. During 16th century, blue was the paper color favored some Italian artists. In the 18th century, some art worked on gray, off-white, and chamois-colored pap

14

TECHNIQUES

A ANGELICO. *The
nunciation*. 1430-35.
ado Museum, Madrid.
mpera holds the place of
nor in the evolution of
inting techniques during
e 15th century in Italy.
ward the end of that cen-
ry, however, tempera
gan to give way to the
st experiments in oils.
like oil painting, in
nich paint can be blended
the surface, tempera
es not allow the artist to
ely blend pigments on
e surface. Rather, each
ade must be mixed
parately, then applied to
own area on the surface.
nnini said: "Continue
e this (using different
lors, one after another)
aking them stand out,
en merging them again,
licately blending them."

I t is not our intention to explain in great detail all of
the techniques used in painting. That alone would
take a large and specialized book. Here we will
deal with the more widespread techniques and the
periods in which they were commonly used. These
techniques vary within certain wide divisions. Artists
painting in those times had their own techniques, well
documented and easy to see today, but jealously
guarded as their very own during their working life.

In prehistoric times, people used iron-based pigments
(coloring materials) to get red, and manganese-based
pigments to get black. Charcoal, and occasionally blood
or casein (a product made from sour milk) were used.
These were all mixed with animal fat, which brought
the pigments together into a primitive "paint."

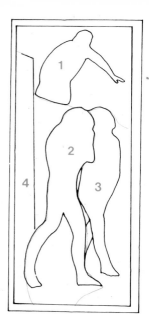

MASACCIO. *The Expulsion from Paradise.* **1424-25. Brancacci Chapel, Santa Maria del Carmine, Florence.**
Fresco is the most widely used technique in wall painting. It is based on a very accurate drawing that gives the artist no margin for error. As a rule, it was used for the great Gothic or Renaissance "narrative" paintings and for the "decorative" work of the Baroque and Rococo periods. As in tempera, the fresco technique requires that the artist work on specific areas in sequence. We can see exactly how much of the fresco was done in each work session.

Fresco lends itself to precise line work, rather than smooth and vibrant brushwork. While an artist is influenced by many factors—materials, setting, ideology, and fashion—the technique used has the greatest bearing on his finished work.

ANONYMOUS. *Proculus the Baker and His Wife.* 1st century. San Martino National Museum, Naples, Italy.
Encaustic painting, used in Rome and Egypt, is beautifully demonstrated in this portrait. It is a fine example of the versatility of an artistic technique used in a certain period.

Tempera, fresco, and encaustic painting were techniques used by the ancient Egyptians, Greeks, and Romans. There are many forms of **tempera** that were used for mural painting. In Egypt, the pigments were mixed with water and gums, size (a gluey substance), and both the whites and the yolks of eggs. Then the pigments were applied to the surface separately, with blending of the colors.

A mixture of egg yolk and the milky sap from the fig tree was used by the great Italian painters of the 14th and 15th centuries. This mixture was sometimes added to frescos to create a mixed, more subtle effect.

A **fresco** is painted onto a base of lime-based plaster using various water-soluble pigments. Mineral-based colors are preferred: St. John's white and slaked lime for whites; natural and burnt ochres for yellows and reds; various earth pigments for reds and greens; lapis lazuli for blue; burnt sienna for browns; and burnt ivory, bone, or coal for blacks. A great deal of advance preparation is required for a fresco. First, a sinopia

17

ANONYMOUS. *Casa Masferrer Sgraffiti.* **Middle of the 18th century. Sant Sadurni d'Osormort.**
Sgraffito has been a widely used decorative method for murals from the Renaissance to the present day. The use of a sketch gives the work a drawinglike appearance. The characters look as though they are in negative form. It is used mostly to decorate, but also to explain historical events and to create images. This work shows the symbolic and decorative use of sgraffito.

JAN VAN EYCK. *The Arnolfini Marriage.* **1434. National Gallery, London, England.**
The invention of oil paint has been credited, more by tradition than fact, to van Eyck, though it was used by Flemish painters in the 15th century. Italian artist Giorgio Vasari described the advantages of oils this way: "The discovery of oil paints was a most fortunate development for the art of painting. They enhance the brilliance of the colors and require only dedication and loving care. Oil makes the colors softer, sweeter, and more delicate, easier to blend

(an accurate drawing) is made on the plaster. It esta lishes the outlines and marks out the individual stag of the work. Dry fresco is a process in which pigmer are applied to a nearly dry wall, then the painting finished with color that is mixed with limewater.

The origins of fresco can be found in the ancie cultures of the Near East and the Mediterrane civilizations of Crete, Greece, and Rome. Examp have also been found in China and India. Fresco beca an important technique in Byzantium, however. importance grew during the Romanesque, Gothic, a Renaissance periods. Early examples of fresco inclu the Romanesque paintings in the Catalonian Pyrene In Italy, Giotto was using the technique in the 14 century, Masaccio in the 15th, and Michelangelo in t 16th. Goya was an outstanding 19th-century master fresco. In Mexico, Diego Rivera and Orozco used fres for huge murals.

Some other forms of mural painting look som what like fresco, but they never achieve its uniq appearance. Oil paints and many of today's mode pigments are now used in wall decoration. Each art has his or her own technique.

Encaustic painting uses pigments dissolved in melt wax and applied to a surface while hot. Evidence this type of painting can still be seen on the fronts

d shade, allowing artists
give their figures a grace,
iveness, and splendor

that cause them to appear
as if in relief, standing free
of the canvas—especially

when done with careful
design, skill, and good
taste."

19

ANTONI TÀPIES.
Grafitti. **1985. Private
Collection.**
Modern artists incorporate
many of the old methods,
but use them to give a
modern message. Pictorial
art is not only the interaction of form and content.
Its techniques, too, have
intrinsic value.

some Doric temples. Usually, however, encaus
paintings are on small, specially prepared wood
panels.

Sgraffito is another decorative mural techniq
The process is simple. Colored plaster is put on
surface, much like the one used for fresco painti
On top of that, two layers of a thin white plas
are applied. Next, the outlines of the subject are draw
and then cut through to the undercoat so that a tw
color effect is achieved. Often put on building from
sgraffito dates back to Renaissance times. It was us
in the 18th century and is still used today as a decorati
feature on neoclassical buildings.

Oil painting is by far the best-known techniq
and is used on wood panels or on canvas. Pigments a
ground and mixed with oil, usually linseed or waln
oil. Although Jan van Eyck is credited for its "inventio
he did not really invent it, for the technique was w
known from ancient times. Van Eyck and oth
15th-century Flemish painters, however, used o

husiastically. Oil painting has many advantages—
rticularly the brilliance of its colors and the ability it
es artists to make changes by superimposing brush
okes. With oils, artists have much greater freedom
action. But any corrections made with oils do become
ible with the passage of time. From the 16th century
, oil painting has become more and more popular. It
s been modified to meet the needs of different artists
d styles of painting.

Contrast the almost flat colors of van Eyck with the
ore rounded figures of Rubens. Van Eyck removed
ty substances from the oil in which he mixed his
ments. Rubens used a thickened oil to which he had
ded turpentine and a soft resin varnish, sometimes
en a beeswax. Today, most painters use prepared oil
int that is sold in tubes, which became widely avail-
le in the 1860s.

Another technique uses **acrylic paints**, which are
ter-based, very flexible, and dry quickly (unlike
s). Also unlike oil paints, acrylics are highly resistant
atmospheric contamination.

In **collage**, various materials—photographs, news-
per cuttings, even solid objects—are used to form a
mposition, which is sometimes affixed to an oil or
rylic base. **Kineticism** tries to reproduce movement
a composition. It introduces additional elements

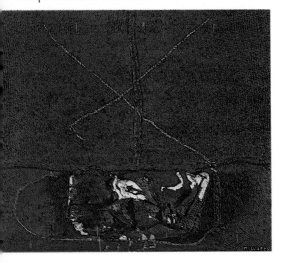

MANUEL MILLARES.
Manikin. **1962. Private
Collection.**
Millares achieves the tex-
tures and tensions of
composition with his
collage of torn sackcloth.
The impact of his work is
enhanced by his use of
white, black, and some red.
He shuns classical brush-
work and seeks communi-
cation through broken,
complex forms. His work
expresses his deep despair.
His forms are a coarse
imitation of reality.
Reality does not exist for
Millares—all that exists is a
sense of dehumanization.

LUIS PARET Y ALCÁZAR. *The Go-Between and the Lovers.* 1784. **Private Collection.**

Watercolor painting has many possibilities but, as with pastel painting, it demands that the artist have great technical skill and a vast knowledge of the medium used. Its rediscovery in the 18th century put it at the same level as the more traditional media. Watercolor painting is a technique that has enjoyed varying popularity. It is not used often by well-known artists, but is used mostly by so-called watercolorists, who are true specialists in their art. Watercolorists today tend to use the white base (surface) as an essential part of the painting's composition.

and technical objects. It also uses tricks of perspect and optical illusion.

One well-known decorative technique uses lacqu Originally from China, **lacquering** was introduced Europe in the 17th century. It became more extensiv used in the 18th century for furniture decoratio Lacquer is a hard, shiny varnish made from the s found in certain trees.

There is continuous interaction between painti and drawing. Generally speaking, a drawing is t first stage of a work of art—a sketch, a plan, or outline of a proposed painting, called a cartoon—a has always been executed with relative speed. Fro the 18th century on, however, drawing was regard as an artistic achievement in its own right. Talent drawing has always been recognized in China a Japan, where the term *hua* denotes painting, drawir

MAURICE QUENTIN DE LA TOUR. *Portrait of Madame Pompadour.* **The Louvre, Paris.**
By the 18th century, pastel had become established as an art form in its own right, especially in France. Maurice Quentin de la Tour was admitted to the French Royal Academy because of a series of pastel portraits he submitted. A certain artificial air, in keeping with the elaborate fashions of 18th century literature, characterizes his work. Pastel is versatile and well suited to more spontaneous and less carefully drawn creations. Here, however, we see what can be achieved with pastel by a skilled artist with a thorough knowledge of the technique.

calligraphy as artistic elements of equal merit
value.

orks on paper have different names according to
echnique used. The most common techniques are
il, charcoal, and red chalk (known as sanguine).
re also are pastel, wax, watercolor, and gouache.

astel is a dry technique. The pigments are ground,
ed with an adhesive, and formed into small sticks.
est feature is the velvety texture that it leaves. But
easily smudged and can be affected by sunlight
humidity. Pastel was widely used in the 18th
ury, particularly by artists in France. More recently,
el has been used by Degas and Picasso.

ax is greasier than pastel. Pigments are dissolved
ax and other meltable substances, then are made
small sticks similar to those of pastel. Wax colors
vivid and adhere well to paper.

ANONYMOUS. *Baptism of Christ.* **6th century. Ariani Baptistery, Ravenna, Italy.**
Mosaic is one of the most widely appreciated artistic techniques. Figures and decorative drawing are done in the artistic styles of the period in which the mosaics were designed. Sometimes mosaics reproduce actual paintings. For example, the mosaics in the basilica of Saint Peter's, Rome, faithfully copy the original of Poussin's *Martyrdom of Saint Erasmus.* The Near East, Rome, and, above all, Byzantium have left us many fine examples of mosaic work. Because it is durable, mosaic gives us some idea of paintings done at the same time—paintings that have long since disappeared.

Watercolor painting uses pigments that are together by gum arabic and thinned with water. effect of light is achieved by the tone of the backgro without the use of any white pigment. Therefore support of a watercolor painting is very impor to its artistic effect.

Gouache differs from watercolor in that white ment is added to the colored pigments. The addi of white gives the paint an opaque effect that is seen in watercolor painting. Gouache was first use the illuminated pages of medieval manuscripts was most widely used in France and England in 18th and 19th centuries.

No overview of techniques would be comp without mentioning gilding, enameling, stained g and mosaic. **Gilding**—the application of gold le gold powder to a surface—was used as a backgro on some paintings of the Gothic and pre-Renaissa periods. The skill, however, goes back much furt to ancient China, India, and Persia, as well as Eg Greece, and Rome. The high price of gold has preve it from being widely used today. Imitation gild using paint, is pointless, for the paint soon tarnish

There are many forms of **enameling**. The t generally describes a glassy coating fused to porce or metal. Enameling was most popular during Gothic period and is still widely practiced today the 18th century, enameling was used to deco jewelry, clocks, snuffboxes, and the like.

Stained glass and mosaics, like the enameling decoration of ceramics, are based on the use of fi techniques. They are included here because composition, design, and decoration are often the w of painters.

These then are the most commonly used media techniques. They have influenced the work of th artists who have used and developed them. Art choose their media and techniques carefully in or to enhance the artistic message they want to conve

THE ELEMENTS OF FORM

When we look at any picture, the first things we see are images with distinct shapes. They may be realistic or they may be abstract. We try to recognize elements within the picture and then to evaluate them. This is when we may confuse physical reality with artistic reality. Abstract art emphasizes pure form and has encouraged people to appreciate form for its own sake. Some shapes are best suited to drawing, or linear depiction, and some to a brush technique.

An emphasis on line, or linear technique, has normally been used in, and been associated with, highly intellectual types of art. In those types of art, artists base their work on ideas rather than on trying to affect the viewer's senses. It is, therefore, not surprising to find works where the line is the basic element binding the separate parts together into geometric shapes.

ERDINAND LEGÉR. *Homage to Jacques-Louis David*. 1948-49. Museum f Modern Art, Paris.

his line drawing clearly lustrates the feeling of the vork. It suggests a concise, lear, sharp, and strong tructure. It encloses each f the elements, leaving hem individual and a part f the whole at the same ime. The artist uses the ne instead of the spontaneous brush stroke.

FRANS HALS. *Gypsy Girl.* **1628-30. The Louvre, Paris.**

The Dutch painter Frans Hals shows the value of loose brushwork. His paintings communicate to the viewer through their spontaneity and are vital, dynamic, and expressive. In this way, he shows a clear relationship between content and artistic language. On the other hand, open or **pictorial form** occurs when the artist expresses himself or herself with a much freer form. An example of an abstract artist who uses this form is Jackson Pollock, who relies on sensual appeal.

This is characteristic of Renaissance, Neo-Classicism, Cubist, and Rationalist paintings.

Shapes can be decorative or speculative. Decorative shapes add many elements to the formal structure of a composition. These elements contribute to any work of art. A picture of a king will have a lot of ornamental elements suitable for a king. These elements may be overemphasized or reduced to a minimum.

Throughout history, artists have created works in which shapes themselves have become the real subjects of the pictures. What is interesting in these works is not the theme, but the shapes making up that theme.

We have talked about tools, supports, and techniques, without talking about elements. The genius of the artist, Velázquez, for example, is that he can

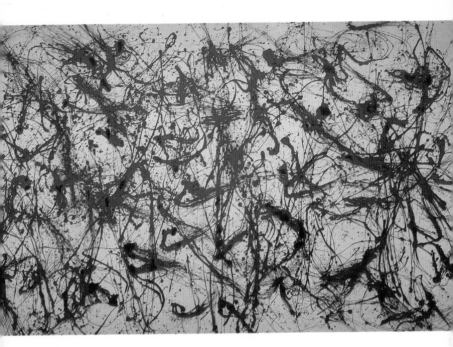

JACKSON POLLOCK.
No. 32. 1950.
Kunstsammlung
Nordrhein Westfalen,
Dusseldorf, West
Germany.

In this work, line takes on an expressive value but is used in a completely new way. Paint has been dripped or smeared onto a canvas lying on the ground. The artist worked from all sides, calling it **action painting**. Pollock's treatment of space is quite new. The viewer is aware of both the surface of the work, and of drips of paint that seem to float in space behind the surface. The picture has no traditional perspective.

MARIANO FORTUNY.
The Spanish Wedding.
1870. Museum of Modern Art, Barcelona.
The freedom that artists used throughout the 19th century is best illustrated in the work of painters such as Meissonier of France and Fortuny. The frivolous style is appropriate to its subject matter. It is far from a sturdy realism.

combine the essential with what might be called added detail.

All works of art can be reduced to geometrical shapes. The structure of these shapes is basic and the painter forgets it at his or her own risk. The circle, the square, the triangle, the rhomboid, the prism, and the cube are all shapes in the elements of a picture. Some painters emphasize them; others hide them beneath lots of details. Artists also use straight and curved lines. The straight line gives a feeling of stability when used

ertically or horizontally. A diagonal line gives energy
o a subject. A curve is always dynamic, except when
 forms a circle. Then it conveys great stability. The
traight line expresses security; the curve usually
xpresses instability.

   The proportion, or balance, between the various
lements is important. When it is applied to the human
gure, this proportion is called a canon, or general
rinciple. The head is most frequently the basic unit
or human proportion. In ancient Egyptian art, there

PETER PAUL RUBENS.
The Three Graces.
**1636-38. Prado Museum,
Madrid.**
An ideal of beauty runs
through the works of many
great artists. In *The Three
Graces*, women are symbols
of physical beauty and also
examples of the changing
taste of each age. The
rounded beauties of
Rubens contrast with the
slim figures of the Italian
painter Botticelli. Both
artists, however, reflect the
style and the ideas of
their age.

e paintings that seem to use the middle finger as a sic unit of measurement.

The Renaissance theorist Alberti established that e ideal height of a person should be equal to 7½ nes the height of his or her head. Alberti based is ratio on studies of real human beings. Dürer :perimented with figures having a height ratio of 7, 8, and 10 heads. The Mannerists distorted the classical le to, in extreme cases, ratios of 1:11 or even 1:12.

DVARD MUNCH. *The cream.* 1893. National ;allery, Oslo, Norway. 'he curved line is the link 1 all so-called Expres- ionist art. Munch, by means of a curved line, defines perfectly an agitated and anguished state of mind. The feeling of emotional instability is shown by the distortion of the figures and shapes. The shape itself is full of ex- pressive meaning. In Munch's work, it is hard to distinguish between form and content, because his method is the meaning.

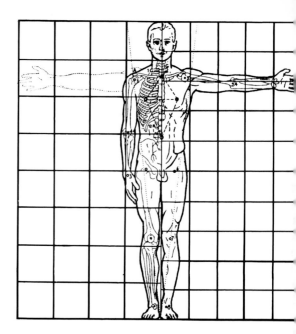

Proportions of the Human Body

PARMIGIANINO. *The Madonna with the Long Neck*. 1531. Uffizi Gallery, Florence.
The golden rule of proportion has changed throughout the history of art. A ratio of 1:8—total body height equals the height of eight heads—was most widely used as a classical norm, although this was modified in the 16th century. Any change from the rule has great significance. Elongation, or lengthening, of the human figure gives it a certain majesty, but also a feeling of insecurity.

Ideals of beauty are not expressed only by the general rule, but take many forms. In *The Three Graces*, in which women represent physical and spiritual beauty, the painter expresses his aesthetic taste, or sense of beauty. For example, the figures in the works of Botticelli, Raphael, and Rubens have come to represent the aesthetic norm of the 14th, 15th and 16th centuries.

Saint Augustine said, "All that exists must have form." We would add that the basic element in a picture is shape, whether it is representational (realistic) or abstract.

32

THE STRUCTURE
OF A WORK

n early type of per-
pective, or viewpoint,
lowed the main element
dominate the upper half
a composition. Each
gure has its planned place
a work, and the way in
hich figures are placed
etermines their relative
nportance in the whole.
aving the figures look in
any directions creates a
veliness in an imaginary
pace.

Shapes acquire a meaning in space. This meaning gives structure to a composition. Artists must arrange all of their elements so that they fulfill their function in the picture. It is this arrangement of shapes that determines the value of a work of art.

Artistic language is complex and is always changing, but it obeys a certain logic. If that logic is not followed, the viewer will not respond.

RAPHAEL. *The School of Athens.* **1512. Stanza della Segnatura, Vatican Palace, Rome, Italy.**

The School of Athens is one of the best examples of the logical arrangement of objects in space as they would appear in reality. The artificial, or scientific, perspective with its converging lines arranges the composition so that the different elements take on their correct dimensions in the picture. The **central vanishing point**—the focus of all the lines of perspective—orders the whole

layout. The architectural features follow these lines, allowing the eye to appreciate the composition. This is the application of the Renaissance definition o perspective: each elemen is of a size corresponding to the position it occupie

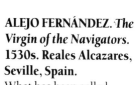

ALEJO FERNÁNDEZ. *The Virgin of the Navigators.* **1530s. Reales Alcazares, Seville, Spain.**

What has been called hierarchical or theological perspective emphasizes the most important figures. We see the Virgin welcoming into her protection the members of the Navigators' Guild (one of them is supposed to be Christopher Columbus) who appear small in comparison with the main figure. This proportion, emphasizing the

Painters must know the rules, absorb them, ar forget them. Only then can they develop their ow individual languages—their styles—which will di tinguish them from other artists. Throughout t history of art, tastes have changed and aesthetic conflic have been frequent. The art of each movement has be analyzed separately. For example, Gothic art mu be evaluated differently than Romantic art.

One of the main aspects of the composition of painting is the distribution of the elements in space that the viewer is completely satisfied. In much of t art of Western cultures since the Renaissance, t viewer looks at a work as if through a window (t picture frame) and does not see an exact representatic of reality, but rather a new reality—artistic reality.

Perspective allows us to position objects in space following our intuition or experience. Artistic pe spective has developed in many ways and has bee influenced by philosophy, religion, and society.

For primitive artists, space was god-given, and the did not impose their own ideas onto it. Foregroun and background were defined according to th

sitioning of figures. Subjects were put on the
rface without any particular order, though at times,
agonally placed figures created a sort of accidental
rspective. The Romans positioned their figures in
more ordered fashion. Each figure was to go in its
vn place according to a plan. Horizontal or vertical
le-by-side position made up the composition, and
e main figure occupied the upper part of the picture.
ligious influence is clearly present in this style.
ace is arranged to express the idea that a distance
ists between humans and the divine. The Gothic
riod introduced the idea of theological perspective.
od the Father, Christ, and the Virgin Mary are
presented as larger than saints and angels, with
man beings shown as the smallest of all.

This medieval hierarchy, or order, was abandoned
ring the Renaissance. Humans became the center

central figure, replaces
reality with an idea and is
used for narrative effect.

ANONYMOUS. *Oxen
trampling grain.* **Valley
of the Kings. Tomb of
Menna, Thebes, Egypt.**
This uses an almost child-
like perspective if we judge
by reality. The worker is not
on top of a mountain of
wheat, but in the middle of
a wheat field. With this
interpretation, the pres-
ence of the oxen, placed
diagonally and in the foreground, is easier to
understand. The painting
is the graphic represen-
tation of a moment.
Although it sometimes
comes near to visual reality,
the painting never dupli-
cates it. Artistic reality has
many forms, which is one
reason it makes it such an
interesting subject
for study.

DIEGO VELÁZQUEZ.
The Maids of Honor (Las Meninas). 1656. Prado Museum, Madrid.

PABLO PICASSO. *The Maids of Honor (Las Meninas)*. 1957. Picasso Museum, Barcelona.
Velázquez's ideas on artistic reality are very clearly expressed in this picture. He uses traditional perspective, to which he has added an imaginative perspective. Thus he creates new or artistic space in which the elements of the picture do not appear to match physical reality.

There are many questions: What exactly is the artist painting? Where are the king and queen? What role does the princess play in her group of attendants? Velázquez has brought together a number of people and elements and implied others. Here we

have one of the most imaginative works in the history of art. Its great merit is that we can enjoy it without understanding all its subtleties. This was the reason Picasso reinterpreted the painting in the best way he knew—with pictorial shapes.

36

ALBRECHT DÜRER. Tools to Duplicate Perspective. 1525. Mechanical and mathematical means were used and described by Dürer. The *fixed viewfinder* allowed the artist to observe the subject through a lens, to trace its outline, and to transfer it to paper by means of a grid, which divided the image into a number of squares. The other system illustrated is the *viewfinder*. It allowed the artist to see his subject through a lens placed between him and it.

and the measure of all things. There was no longer any need to show the difference between the earthly and the spiritual. Space was distributed according to the human figures shown. Artists created perspective in which they sized people and objects in relation to their position within the picture.

We can see the development of perspective in the 14th century. Artists created three-dimensional space while representing reality, although there was no formal perspective. In the 15th century, artists' status grew with the invention and use of scientific perspective.

CANALETTO. *View of the Church of the Salute and Entrance to the Grand Canal, Venice.* **1730. The Louvre, Paris.**

The *camera obscura* was a basic tool of the **veduta painters**—painters of places, usually towns. True depiction of a landscape takes for granted the use of some optical device to prevent any error. The **camera obscura** is a small, portable box with a circular hole in the top. In the box is a lens carrier. The lens can be moved up or down in the carrier, changing the distance between the lens and the flat base of the box, where the paper is placed. On the lens carrier, a

Painting changed from being the work of a craftsperso to the work of an artist. **Pictorial space**, in which ar point could be taken as the center, was created. Usual a central perspective view was presented, in which th horizon coincided with the vanishing point.

Many theories were developed during the Renaissan to explain techniques of perspective. In central Europ practical and theoretical studies did not appear un the 16th century, although similar solutions had bee found by painters in the previous century.

Jan van Eyck, using a mirror, obtained curve perspectives, as he showed in *The Arnolfini Marriag* Roger van der Weiden, although he did not use scientific perspective system, obtained lifelike result

By the end of the 15th century and the beginning the 16th century, the theories and practice of perspecti had been developed. New ways to organize space ha been widely exchanged among artists. **Color pe spective** appeared—suggesting a movement into spac with the use of lighter tones toward the back of picture. Color perspective was used alone or wi linear perspective. Venetian painters favored a colo

movable, inclined mirror captures the image and projects it onto the paper, where it is traced by the painter. This direct process has now been replaced by slides that the artist projects directly onto canvas. The painter chooses the landscape. Then, by using light and color, he or she introduces atmospheric factors that the camera obscura cannot capture.

stem, and the Florentines used the single vanishing oint as their means of organizing space. Leonardo da inci, working in Florence, wrote: "The science of ainting includes all the colors of the base and the rms of the bodies that take on these colors, together ith their proportions, according to whether they are ear to or far away. This is the mother of perspective, y which I mean the science of the lines of vision, a ience that may be divided into three parts: the first icludes the linear construction of the bodies [linear erspective], the second, the change in color in relation distance [perspective of color], and the third, the

ANDREA POZZO. *False Cupola.* **1685. Church of San Ignatius, Rome.**

In the works of the Jesuit painter Andrea Pozzo, visual trickery comes very close to the illusions found in Baroque art. This illusion of a cupola should be viewed from the entrance to the church. Pozzo does not support the idea of multiple vanishing points. His vanishing point is both geometrical and symbolic. Pozzo wrote that "the task of the painter is to draw all the lines ... to the real focus point, that of Divine glory."

ANONYMOUS. *Christ and the Apostles.* End of the 12th century. Diocese of Urgel. Museum of Catalan Art, Barcelona.
Seeking harmony of composition, the artist has arranged his elements to the right and the left of a central axis. He applies the rule of perfection in which two of the fundamental points are harmony and symmetry. The figure of Christ occupies the center. The apostles, in two groups of six, face inward on either side. In theory, if we were to fold the picture down its central axis, the group on the right would exactly match the figures on the left.

loss of sharpness of the image, also in relation distance [diminishing perspective]."

In this period of transition between the order of th 15th century and the disorder of the 16th, artists beg using a **perspective of illusion**, in which optical trick make us see things that do not really exist.

Creating the illusion of spaces involves the use multiple vanishing points. Mantegna introduces us multiple vanishing points with his decoration of th *Nuptial Bed* in the Ducal Palace at Mantua. He use greatly foreshortened figures to suggest a deep fie of view.

Venetian painters, in composing their great work used several vanishing points arranged around a centr axis, or imaginary line. At times, the vanishing poin were outside the painting, which created the effect great energy. Because painters want to make the compositions believable, they must sometimes chang the strict rules of perspective. For example, the Man nerists knew the rules, but broke them because of th needs of their particular art and, thus, produced som surprising results.

n the 17th century, many artists questioned the
ues that, at the time, formed the basis of all scientific
ught. German astronomer Johannes Kepler's theory
s that parallel lines meet in the infinite. The infinite
peared as illusory space. It is not surprising, then,
t rules began to evolve for illusion, although it had
en in common use since the end of the 15th century.
roque art of the 17th century, however, sought the
inite, the undefined. Decoration of walls, vaults,

TINTORETTO. *The*
Washing of the Feet. **1547.**
Prado Museum, Madrid.
Mannerism broke with the
traditional symmetrical
axis, which coincided with
a central vanishing point.
Tintoretto foreshortened
diagonal perspective and
fanned out his figures,
widening the field of vision.
Here we see a composition
with a deep field of view. It
is created by background
architectural features and
delicate areas of light and
shade.

RUGINO. *The Delivery*
the Keys. **1480-82.**
stine Chapel, Rome.
en at the height of the
naissance, Perugino con-
ued to follow the idea
at the center is the most

important spot in a com-
position. He arranged his
groups around a theo-
logical center—in this case
the key, symbol of the
Papacy. The key, placed on
the axis of symmetry, is the

point around which the
whole painting revolves.
Groups, rather than the
individual, predominate.

41

FRANCISCO ZURBARÁN.
Still Life. 1633. Prado
Museum, Madrid.

The artist emphasized the
individual, rather than the
group. The composition
singles out the objects,
placing them side by side,
rather than one in front of
another. The painting can
be divided into separate
parts, each of which has its
own value and interest. It is
unlike those compositions
in which individual ele-
ments are important only
because of their association
with others.

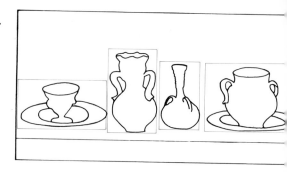

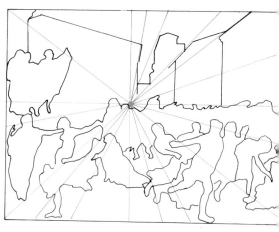

NICOLAS POUSSIN. *The
Rape of the Sabines.*
1637-38. The Louvre,
Paris.

This is an outstanding
example of centralized
composition. Poussin
creates a deep, open space,
and places his figures

within lines radiating out
from the center of the picture toward infinity. This
type of open composition
gives a dynamic quality to
the whole. It creates a series

of emotional tensions. In
this way, the meaning and
the dramatic effect of the
work come from the com-
bination of visual style and
formal composition.

and ceilings tried to create integral space. Column
were severely foreshortened and designs were mad
so figures could be painted on curved surfaces, suc
as domed ceilings, and still appear lifelike when viewe
from a proper position.

In easel painting, **aerial perspective**—a subtl
combination of color and shade—is used. The element
of a picture are defined in space by the use of light an
color.

The 17th-century style of Baroque continued int
the 18th with the introduction, in Venice, of veduta

MASACCIO/MASOLINO.
The Virgin and Child with
Saint Anne. 1424. Uffizi
Gallery, Florence.
Enclosed compositions are
based on a central line or
axis. All elements group
around this theoretical
central area in which the
main figure is placed. In
this picture, medieval symmetry is used with a theological center. A certain
"humanizing" of the figures
gives the work a modern
feeling.

TOINE WATTEAU.
les. 1717-19.
e Louvre, Paris.
e artist shows his
jects in different ways,
h the viewer in mind.
e line of the horizon is
d to give meaning to the
work. A low horizon gives
the figure greater prom-
inence. Watteau uses a
clown, rather than a king or
saint, as his main character.
He gives this traditional
figure of fun a grandeur.

duta is a style that brought science and nature
ser together. Algorotti wrote: "Painters will have to
e the optical camera in the same way that astronomers
e the telescope and physicists the microscope. All
se instruments lead to a better understanding of
ure." The camera obscura reproduced perspective
the same way as a modern photographic camera.
Painters today still use traditional techniques of
rspective. **Flat perspective**, in which the elements
a picture are juxtaposed (placed side by side), is also
mmonly used. It is linked to the use of different
wpoints (in Cubism) or of color (in Impressionism).

43

PETER PAUL RUBENS.
Rustic Dance. 1630.
Prado Museum, Madrid.
In painting, the *dynamics of space* almost always means the blending of the various

parts into a whole. The use of the curved line and the open, fluid brush technique help tie the composition into a whole. They are complementary elements, used

individually. In this work Rubens seeks an overall, rather than a particular, effect.

The New Realists, using camera and transparencie promoted what is called photographic perspective.

Composition in painting emphasizes the blending of elements into a whole. The idea of symmetry, balance, is important. Early painters established symmetrical axis and placed elements in an order way to the left and the right of this axis. Romant and Gothic artists stressed this organization and repeated elements in an identical manner. Renaissance artists, however, tended to balance space with group of figures. Renaissance technique, then, resulted in

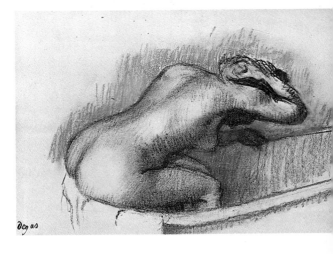

GAR DEGAS. *La ...lette.* **1896. Musée ...rsay, Paris.**
...some of his work, Degas ...ated his subjects as ...ply elements of the ...mposition. He pursued ...ions of reality that are ...ser to photography ...an to painting. His ...rupt viewpoints were ...vel. They tended to ...sen the importance of ... subject.

...eater individuality for both figures and objects, all ...which then had their own personalities.

Mannerist artists organized space in an irregular ...ay. At first look, Mannerist space might appear dis-...ganized, but it is never unbalanced. It is a kind of ...mmetrical asymmetry. Although it shows itself in ...fferent ways, balance is critical to all painting.

Symmetry is closely linked to different types of ...mpositions. **Enclosed composition** is normally ...ased on a central line or axis—all elements are associ-...ed with the theoretical center of the picture. It is ...pical of the medieval and Renaissance works.

JUAN VAN DER HAMEN. *Still Life.* **The National Gallery of Art, Washington, D.C., U.S.A.**
The use of a high horizon seems to put all the elements on display individually. With a raised horizon line, the forms in the picture appear to lean toward the viewer, as they would if set out on a market stall. Thus, the viewer dominates the scene.

PERUGINO. *Virgin and Child with Four Saints.* 1479. Vatican Museum, Rome.
This work clearly shows the importance of the horizon. It is at midheight in relation to the four saints, but it is low for the Virgin Mary on her throne. The saints are set at the same level as the viewer, with the Virgin higher and thus more important. This technique adds force to the work.

An **open composition** may have elements arranged around a central or a lateral (side) axis, or with external vanishing point. It is a composition in which the elements appear out of place, off center, and sometimes even left out of the painting. This was particularly done by Mannerist and Baroque artists. As a general rule, enclosed compositions unite elements, open compositions break apart elements.

PETER PAUL RUBENS. *The Raising of the Cross.* 1609-10. Antwerp Cathedral, Antwerp, Belgium.
This is a complex work. To obtain a dynamic space, the artist used both a diagonal line and a curved S-pattern. The result is a scene of great tension, matching the event portrayed.

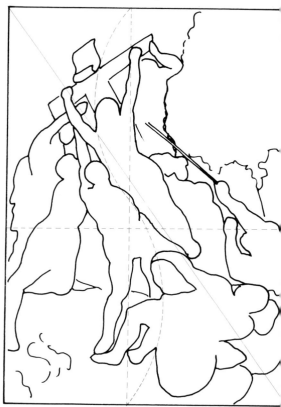

LUCA SIGNORELLI.
Holy Family. **1480. Uffizi Gallery, Florence.**
Here the circle dictates the composition of the whole work, which is made to fit into the framework. The artist set up a gentle rhythm. He linked the bowed posture of Joseph with that of the Virgin Mary. The picture has a significant theoretical center point: the Christ Child.

A composition may be unified or nonunified. In a fied picture, elements interact and are superimposed each other. In a nonunified picture, elements are taposed and individualized.

n a unified work, the artists emphasize the whole nposition. They do not emphasize one part at the pense of the whole. This is typical of Baroque works. nunified composition deals with objects and figures re separately. In the Realist works, figures and ects are essential elements in composition. Unified l nonunified composition can provide either great rity or great obscurity. Individual objects are easier understand than a general overall effect, but the

47

RUDOLF VON ES.
Nativity. **1370. Library, Munich, West Germany.**
The golden section, or divine proportion, was widely used during the Renaissance. Within a rectangle, divided into two equal parts, a new space is created based on the arc of a circle with its center on the midpoint of the longest side. The artist has placed the reclining Virgin within the arc, helping us to visualise the layout.

fewer individual elements or details a picture has, easier it is to understand.

A very important aspect of composition in perspec is the location of the horizon. Elements are not pla in relation to the horizon merely to please the eye, to add emphasis to the content of the work. Anyth placed on or above the horizon becomes more portant and tends to dominate the work. Objects be the line of the horizon appear smaller and become l important. A high horizon reduces the importanc the subject; a low horizon increases it.

Elements in a painting may be based on the cir the oval, the triangle, the square, or even the penta; or the hexagon. Sometimes these shapes are u

PETER PAUL RUBENS.
Hélène Fourment and Her Children. **1636-37. The Louvre, Paris.**

Rubens's work follows a preestablished plan in which geometry orders whole. The center of th composition is a circle, with the S-shaped lines linking the other eleme smoothly to the princip figures. Baroque freedo was still restricted by geometry, though the curves that predomina here adapt to the gentlen of the whole work.

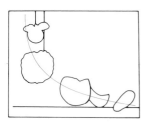

JUAN SÁNCHEZ COTÁN.
Still Life. **1603. Fine Arts Gallery, San Diego, U.S.A.**
This plastic, speculative layout is one of Cotán's most frequently used devices. Structural strength is established by arranging the objects along the arc of

a circle. Here the painter emphasized the laws of geometry, which becam more important than th real appearance of the objects themselves.

EDGAR DEGAS. *Glass of Absinthe*. 1876. Musée d'Orsay, Paris.

Degas is a master in the use of space. This could almost be a photographic approach – the people pushed to the right-hand edge of the composition – but the pictorial value and the zigzag construction confirm the superiority of painting over the mere objectivity of the camera. Degas uses the eye of the photographer but introduces the subjective view of the artist. This is no instant snapshot of the two people. Degas studied them, took in the whole scene, and only then gave us his own interpretation of it. This is the painting's greatest value—it captures an atmosphere, rather than a moment.

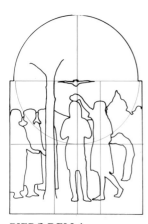

PIERO DELLA FRANCESCA. *The Baptism of Christ.* 1448-50. National Gallery, London.

individually, sometimes together. To give feeling to composition, figures are arranged in straight lines vertical, horizontal, or diagonal—or in curves.

Regular geometrical shapes give a feeling of ord Irregular forms give a feeling of energy and action.

A work of art is not merely the product of form a shape, but of various complementary methods facilitating interpretation. A circle tends to focus t action; curved or diagonal lines give dynamism. wide-based triangle shows stability; an inverted triang shows instability. Geometry forms the basis of pictor

PIERO DELLA FRANCESCA. *Brera Altarpiece.* 1472-76. Brera Art Gallery, Milan, Italy.

In *Baptism of Christ*, Piero della Francesca used geometry to regulate the space. It is divided into three equal parts vertically and two horizontally. Symmetry demands that the tree trunk be placed to the left of center, balancing the figure of John the Baptist on the right. The Holy Spirit occupies a position two-thirds up from the base. It is the center of a circle that takes in the top two-thirds of the picture, and its size is linked to that of John the Baptist's arm. In *Altarpiece of Brera*, the circle dominates the composition, based on a symmetrical axis, and gives it dynamism.

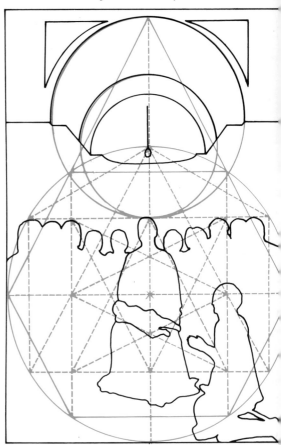

t. A viewer's appreciation of this fact depends upon e number of added details—details that are added th to complement and obstruct the geometrical ucture of a work.

A picture, however, is not just drawing and geometry. has the two essential elements of color and tone.

Colors can be cold (blues and violets) or warm (reds d oranges). Different terms have been used for this uble aspect: positive and negative; active and passive. rtists use color to attract or distance the viewer.

Cold colors are used intellectually. Warm colors, on e other hand, allow the viewer to involve his or her elings. Mannerist artists used cold colors, while enaissance artists used warm colors. Color alone, owever, does not determine a viewer's response to the ainting.

EL GRECO. *Laocoön.* **1610-14. The National Gallery of Art, Washington, D.C.**

The Mannerism of El Greco broke with the warm, glowing colors of the Renaissance by using distant, cold tones. The work is frozen and intellectual, distancing itself from our senses. Both the unreality of proportion and the attitudes of the figures emphasize this distancing.

INCENT VAN GOGH.
lf Portrait with Hat.
87. Stedelijk Museum,
nsterdam, Netherlands.

n Gogh used compli-
entary colors and broken
lor, techniques of the
pressionists, to achieve
brant visual effects. The
pressionists sought to
cord their perceptual
periences—to paint what
ey saw. The startling
minous color in Van
ogh's paintings suggests
at he was recording more
an simply visual truth.
s heightened contrasts
complimentary colors
d his fierce brush
rokes seem to express
turbulent emotional
ate. Van Gogh, like the
pressionists, strove to
cord what he saw, but he
so left us a record of
other kind of truth—the
notions of the artist.

JEAN-FRANÇOIS MILLET. *El Angelus.* 1858-59. Musée d'Orsay, Paris.

A quiet grandeur pervades Millet's *El Angelus.* It expresses a sense of unity, a sense that the man and woman are one with the land and the sky. This effect is achieved, in great part, by Millet's orchestra-tion of the tone relation-ships in the painting. Millet makes the tone move from dark to light in subtle grad-ations. The rhythm set up by this gradual movement can be associated with the dignified rhythms of pro-cessional ceremonies—an association quite unlike what one might expect from the humble subject matter. Compare Millet's painting with the Caravag-gio on page 54. Caravaggio made his dark areas and light areas contrast sharply rather than allowing them to merge with one another, as Millet did. Caravaggio used this high contrast to create visual excitement, an excitement that helps to convey the drama of the subject: the moment of the conversion of Saint Paul on the road to Damascus.

Painters use a harmony of tones that brings a unity color to their work. Paintings that contain com-ementary colors are harmonious, or pleasing and eaceful. The use of contrasting colors can make aintings look active and aggressive.

Impressionist artists followed a rule that color was verything in a painting and that black, the non-color, ust never appear. The Expressionists used black in symbolic way. For instance, they used black to express elings of despair or depression.

Light is also a determining factor in any composition. analyzing a painting or drawing in terms of light it is teresting to note whether it is illuminated by its own

CARAVAGGIO. *The Conversion of Saint Paul.* **1600-01. Santa Maria del Popolo, Rome.**

Artificial light, as used here by Caravaggio, comes from a point outside the composition and is focused on the most significant thematic point. This is divine light, emphasizing the artist's message. The figure of Saint Paul, receiving the Holy Spirit, is dramatically lit, as though on a stage.

...ght. This color/light combination is necessary for ...y composition, since both elements create order ...d space.

Lighting in paintings varies. Renaissance artists used ...tense light in the foreground, but diminished light in

CLAUDE MONET. *Rouen Cathedral−Morning.* **1894. Musée d'Orsay, Paris.**

Light and color can capture a moment. This is imaginative use of color. The cathedral, with all its ornamental Gothic detail, offers ideal variations of light, which is suited to the study of the atmosphere it gives off. Monet was not really trying to paint the cathedral. Instead, he wanted to show, through a series of paintings, the different moods that surround it at different times of day.

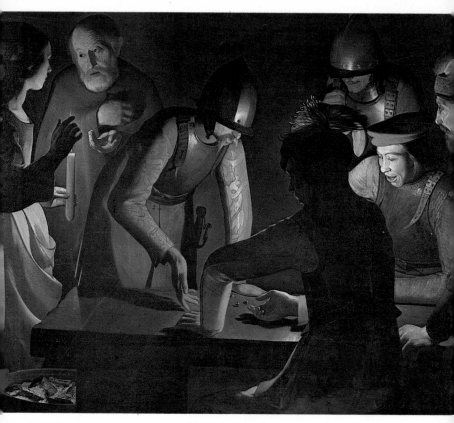

GEORGES DE LA TOUR.
The Denial of Saint Peter.
**1645. Nantes Museum,
Nantes, France.**
Natural light comes from a
candle—a real, identifiable
source. This is often the
case with de la Tour. The
technique is effective. It
allows the artist to outline
each element in the picture
as a whole. It is a formal
use of light, well suited
to imaginative works such
as this.

the background. This is in contrast to the gloom that i
characteristic of Baroque works. In Baroque art, strongi
lit figures emerged from a plain, dark background.

Light can also be used to separate the foregrounc
middle ground, and background of a painting, as i
aerial perspective. Vermeer used dark foreground
with a maximum intensity of light in the background
Depending on how it is distributed, light can be all c
the same kind, dual—in which dark background
emphasize the figures—or mixed.

The light can come either from outside the pictur
or from an identifiable source, such as the candle i
Georges de la Tour's *Denial of Saint Peter*. External ligh
is used in a variety of ways in a composition. It can b
focused or diffused, real or unreal, composite or purel
conceptual.

ACOPO BASSANO.
doration of the
hepherds. **Second half**
f the 17th century. Her
Majesty, The Queen's
Collection. Hampton

Court, London.
The light in this work is symbolic. It comes from the Christ Child and the angels above, and creates an interplay of light and dark.

A similar use of light—from the angel above the tent—is found in Francesca's *The Dream of Constantine* on page 64.

GIOVANNI BELLINI.
Woman Combing Her Hair. **1516.**
Kunsthistorisches Museum, Vienna, Austria.
This late work seems, at first, to have a natural lighting effect, but that is not the case. The window in the background provides no light. It is just perspective space. The artist has abandoned logic and created a totally artificial balance of tones. What we have called pictorial reality is never a faithful representation of physical reality.

The use of light to create shadows is called **chiaroscuro**. The use of more dark area than light area is called **tenebrism**.

Tangible light comes from a light source within the picture—a candle, a torch or a lamp—which gives logical chiaroscuro effect. Raphael and El Greco use this tangible light. Caravaggio, on the other hand, uses an external artificial light source, which throws light on one specific part of the composition.

Diffused light softens the outlines of objects. Some works of Leonardo da Vinci and the Italian artist Correggio illustrate this.

Real light, an almost impossible dream of the painter, has been sought by many artists. For example, Claude Lorrain, painting mostly in Italy during the 17th century, mixed his colors in the fields, matched them against the light effects he saw, and then rushed back to to his studio to work on his painting. The Impressionists

mpleted works in the open air, all the time observing
e effects of light and color. Throughout history,
tists have tried to merge what they see with what
ey paint.

Religious painting, on the other hand, tends to use
ures—the Christ Child, for example—as the source
symbolic light.

Light must be divided into two forms—artistic and
nceptual. Artistic light includes all those forms we

THÉODORE GÉRICAULT. *The Raft of the Medusa.* **1819. The Louvre, Paris.**

The dramatic power of a painting stems from two basic factors—lighting, and the rhythm of the composition itself. Here the artist draws the viewer's attention to the two pieces of cloth, white and red, that the two figures in the top part of the painting are waving. From here, we can follow the whole structural rhythm of the work, based on one diagonal crossed by another (the great sail). Thus, a conflict is created between the desires of the survivors and fate, which seems to be pushing them away from salvation.

ave discussed. Conceptual light tries to emphasize
e message. By the use of light, artists draw attention
the particular area of the composition, which they
ant the viewer to concentrate. This use of light is best
en in the works of Caravaggio, who also emphasizes
is realist message by using artificial light.

All works of art have areas of greater and lesser
mphasis. Such areas are the beginning of a visual
urney that will please the viewer if the distribution
f space, color, and light are satisfactory.

The focal point of a painting, most often a figure,
usually the area of greatest contrast, both of tone
nd of color. The focal point, the rhythm of the com-
osition, the color, and the light are the basis for
nderstanding a work.

ANONYMOUS. *The Goddess Knut, Surrounded by Signs of the Zodiac.* **2nd century. British Museum, London.**

Throughout the history of art, religious themes have always been important. Most civilizations have portrayed their gods. The Egyptians showed them in their tombs and coffins. Here we see Knut, wife of Geb. She is goddess of the heavens and is shown symbolically by the signs of the zodiac. If we do not recognize the character represented, our appreciation is limited to form alone, and the picture will lose some of its meaning.

SALVADOR DALI. *Christ of Saint John of the Cross.* **1951. Kelvingrove Art Gallery and Museum, Glasgow, Scotland.**

Few artists have created religious art since the 19th century. An exception is Dali. This work belongs to the tradition of Spanish realist painting from earlier centuries. Starting from a very modern viewpoint, Dali tries to create a message from Spanish mystical literature. This shows how beliefs of the past can be reinterpreted in modern style. One message has many valid interpretations.

THE MEANING
OF THE WORK

TINTORETTO. *Death of Holofernes*. 1555-79. Prado Museum, Madrid.
Knowledge of the story is necessary for a full understanding of this picture. Both the Old and the New Testaments must be read to understand the religious painting of the Western world. Only if we have this knowledge can we judge whether a picture accurately portrays its message. Here we see an interpretation of the episode in the Old Testament of the Douay Bible when Judith, having called upon God, took hold of the hair of his head ... and smote [struck with a sword] twice upon his neck with all her might, and she took away his head from him." (Jth. 13:7-11)

A painting must be considered as a whole. In it, technique, composition, and content come together to form a work of art.

It is through technique and composition that artists express their beliefs—religious, nonreligious, cultural, or purely artistic. These are expressed visually by themes.

The history of art started with the magical, represented by the paintings of the prehistoric world. Prehistoric artists—primarily hunters—painted images

of animals they wished to capture for food and clothing. Their paintings represented possession, and sometimes their desires became reality. This magical influence surfaces throughout the whole history of art.

Sometimes art is simply decorative. Such art does not claim to be a copy of reality. Instead, real elements are gathered together into a composition which does not tell a story, but is simply an ornament. Such applied

13.

BARTOLOMÉ ESTABAN MURILLO. *The Holy Family with a Bird.* **1650. Prado Museum, Madrid.** Baroque art sentimentalized themes and brought them closer to everyday life. Religious art of the time often depicted saints. Joseph was one of those most frequently shown. This picture displays the realism with which religious themes were treated. At the same time, it shows Joseph as the leading player, with the Virgin Mary placed in the background.

art does not have any real message beyond pleasing the eye.

The major division in themes is between the religious and the secular, or nonreligious. Religious themes are found in the ancient cultures of Egypt, Assyria, Mesopotamia, Persia, and other countries. In very old works from these cultures, the theme mainly exists in sculpture. Paintings from ancient Greece and Rome are usually of secular subjects.

LLUÍS BORRASSÀ.
Resurrection. **1411-18.
Museum of Catalan Art,
Barcelona.**
The Gothic world placed
great value on the symbolic
element of a composition.
Here, the figure of the risen
Christ symbolizes the tri-
umph of religion over
paganism, which is repre-
sented by the sleeping
soldiers. The composition
itself is eloquent and fits
the message of the picture.

Every portrayal of a religious event is interpreted in
different ways. The interpretation depends on two
things: who the artist is, and in what period of history
the portrayal is done. An artist will often put religious
figures in the clothing of his or her own time. This
leads to the variety of ways a subject is treated. Medieval
artists stressed the symbolic character of a person.
Renaissance and Baroque artists sentimentalized the
subject.

Baroque artists used the lives of the saints as examples
of conduct to be imitated. It was the ability to inform

PIERO DELLA FRANCESCA. *The Dream of Constantine.* **1455. Church of San Francesco, Arezzo, Italy.**
Piero della Francesca depicted the story of *The Dream of Constantine* very well on the walls of a church. The sleeping emperor dreams that an angel shows him a cross and says "Under this sign shalt thou conquer."

JOSÉ ANTOLÍNEZ. *The Immaculate Conception.* **1670. Private Collection.** The Virgin is one of the most widely portrayed themes in the history of art. Seventeenth-century artists made her the main figure in many paintings. The heavenly depiction of the figure raises it above the viewer and presents it as a cult object. The figure of the Holy Spirit symbolizes divine conception, and the white lilies represent purity.

d teach that made painting an important art form
uring the Baroque period.

The use of saints as perfect examples is a visual way
expressing the union of chosen souls with God.
ney are models to follow, ideals toward which to
rive.

A list of all the main religious themes would be
xtensive. At various times, images from the New
estament have been linked to various saints. The
irgin Mary, surrounded by saints, was a common
ene in works of the Renaissance period. During the
aroque period, artists introduced, as subject matter,
ne Immaculate Conception. At other times, religion
as been linked to stories of real events—miracles,
pparitions, or martyrdoms of the saints. Sometimes
ne Holy Trinity (Father, Son, and Holy Ghost),
ne Resurrection (of Christ), and the Eucharist

TITIAN. *Charles V at Mühlberg*. 1548. Prado Museum, Madrid.
This is a portrait that has symbolic meaning. We see a physical likeness of the king but, above all, the picture symbolizes the Spanish Catholic monarchy triumphing over th Protestants on the banks of the Elbe.

(communion) are shown. There are many ways depicting these subjects, and they often are interwove into the same painting.

Understanding a religious painting depends on visual attraction and on a recognition of its them Some knowledge of the Christian saints and of the O

peak in 17th-century Flanders. Throughout the history of art, scenes of peasant, middle-class, and upper-class life have been the subjects of paintings in many different styles and interpretations. If we look carefully here, we can see a faithful reproduction of an atmosphere and of various levels of society.

Note here the harmony between the composition of the picture and the personality of the person portrayed. The zigzag lay-out is meant to show the arrogant character of Jean Claude-Richard de Saint-Non, the Abbot of Pothieres. The artist is not so much concerned with symbolism as with the depiction of a strong person, of someone sure of himself. Here, we see the portrayal of an attitude, not descriptive detail.

FRANÇOIS BOUCHER
Miss O'Murphy. **1752.**
Alte Pinakothek, Munich,
West Germany.
We see here the distinction
between a person posing
for a portrait and a model
posing for a pictorial composition. In this painting of
Louise O'Murphy, a young
girl of loose morals,
Boucher reflected the
tastes of a part of French
society of the time. This
single picture sums up an
entire group.

and New Testaments is essential for a comp
understanding of such works.

Secular painting has many thematic styles. On
the portrait. The Romans introduced the idea of port
into painting. However, few examples of their w
have survived, and their portraiture, or portrait mak
is best known through their sculptures. The us
portraits generally disappeared until Gothic times, w
portraits and self-portraits became more commonpl
The basic aim of the portrait was to concentrate o
subject and the many ways in which it could be depic

This individual treatment of a subject includes
family group portrait. Another type of portrait, in wh
the subject is shown with the saints, was done in
Baroque period of the 17th century.

Genre painting depicts realistic scenes from eve
day life. In 17th-century Holland, the middle class a

PAUL CÉZANNE. *Still Life with Apples and Oranges.* **1885-1900. Musée d'Orsay, Paris.** Still life has always had clear links with the society it depicts. Communities reflect daily life through the objects. After the 19th century, objects in such paintings became less symbolic.

VINCENT VAN GOGH. *Sunflowers.* **1888-89. Staat Gallerie, Munich.** Flower paintings have both a decorative and a pictorial value. They represent both the courtly and the middle-class way of life. Flower painters tried to paint their subjects as faithfully as possible, paying great attention to detail. Gradually, they simplified these works. Van Gogh has merely suggested the forms of the sunflowers, using a thick layer of paint to give a feeling of their texture.

ANDRÉ DÉRAIN.
Westminster Bridge. 1905.
Paris.
This is a "pure" landscape,
painted for its own sake,
without figures. It is linked
with the middle class. It
appreciates what it represents. The countryside and
the city frequently com-
peted as subjects for
paintings. The landscape
is an intermediate stage
between the realist works
of the 17th century and the
photography of the 20th
century.

WILLIAM TURNER.
Storm at Sea. 1840. **Tate
Gallery, London.**
Here, Turner does not
depict a seascape, but uses
his canvas to portray a
world of feelings. This is
not a reflection of reality—it
represents an imagined
reality. It is painting in its
purest form.

the aristocracy, or upper class, had themselves portra
in their immediate surroundings so they could
depicted as they lived.

Still life is another theme. Together with flo
painting, it came to prominence in the 16th and 1
centuries. It has a double role: It depicts a society a
is a decoration. It has been one of the most popu
themes during the last three centuries. Impression
artists made it decorative, and Cubist artists used it
a vehicle for the study of forms.

Renaissance artists used landscapes as a complementary or perspective element. Landscape painting
in its own right first appeared in central Europe. In the
7th century, Dutch painters, such as Hobbema,
uysdael, and Vermeer, depicted the landscape in a
ealistic manner, as an expression of their sheer pleasure
n the world around them. In Italy, the French artist
Claude Lorrain used the landscape to capture a mood.
he 18th-century artists in England made the landscape
theme.

DIEGO RIVERA. *Man at the Crossroads Looking with Hope and High Vision to the Choosing of a New and Better Future.* **1934. Palace of Fine Arts, Mexico City, Mexico.** Rivera's mural commemorates the average citizen, daily life, and social change. Rivera was originally commissioned by Nelson Rockefeller in 1932 to paint this mural in New York City's RCA Building. Because Rivera included a portrait of Lenin, Rockefeller had the fresco destroyed before it was completely finished. Rivera re-created the mural in Mexico City on a wall donated by the Mexican government. This particular work depicted an ideal world that was controlled by educated workers. It was a world in which war, as well as religion, was superceded by socialist doctrines. This version of the mural contains portraits not only of Lenin but also of Trotsky, Marx, Engels, and other communist figureheads.

72

Historical themes are related to myths. Paintings that record successful events or efforts are clearly linked to national pride.

Royalty and common people all want the events in which they were the winners to be remembered. Sometimes the desire for personal glory makes an individual the main figure in a work of art. After the Renaissance, this desire to be remembered became very strong and became more evident in artistic works. Use of a low horizon and symbolism increase the importance of the main figure in commemorative art.

PABLO PICASSO.
Guernica. 1936.
**Casón del Buen Retiro,
Madrid.**
Here, the desire to record
an event is turned into an
artistic subject of social
judgment. Picasso depicts
no glory, just the drama of
war. Two aspects need to be
pointed out: the mono-

Mythology has probably been the greatest art them
It has two sides—religious and symbolic. In the ancie
world and in Eastern cultures, mythical gods repr
sented what Christian figures and events represe
during the Middle Ages. The gods were used to illustra
a Christian message, but their use could vary. Historic
and mythological art often carries an assumptic
that the viewer has a detailed knowledge of the subjec

Allegory, which has appeared in art from th
beginning, is the representation of ideas, such as th

74

immaculate Conception, virtue, vice, faith, charity, justice, strength, courage, and cowardice. It is linked to religious painting, but above all, to glorified historical figures. The virtues of the Christian hero are best represented in allegorical form.

Modern painters have experimented with form and have given us nonfigurative representations, which illustrate the purity of art. They have also given us form valid in itself, form with meaning. This can be called imaginative use of form. We should not seek to chrome, or one-color, nature of the picture, which tends to create a certain distance; and the scorn of a dictator, here represented as the executioner of a confused town. When a Nazi official asked who had done the preliminary sketches for *Guernica*, Picasso replied, "You did."

JOAN MIRÓ. *Woman and Birds at Dawn.* 1946. Fundacio Miró, Barcelona.

Miró is a great believer of significant form, a symbolism not easily understood. He moved away from the established language of reality and form, then created his own language within a set of his own rules. The viewer who does not understand Miró's paintings should remember that a person who does not read Chinese will not understand something written in that language. The message is clear, however, to those who do know Chinese.

identify form with reality, but to judge it in its own right.

Painting can only be understood in the framework of culture and thought. This is both its great virtue and its great limitation.

FRANCISCO DE GOYA.
Saturn Devouring His Son.
1819. Prado Museum,
Madrid.

For Goya, the theme here portrays the decadence of a set of social values in which he had once believed. Saturn represents unlimited power, capable of destroying—without feeling—beings whom he himself had created and protected. Spain, in the 19th century, appeared this way to Goya, and he depicted his disillusionment in a thinly veiled disguise.

ART THROUGHOUT THE AGES

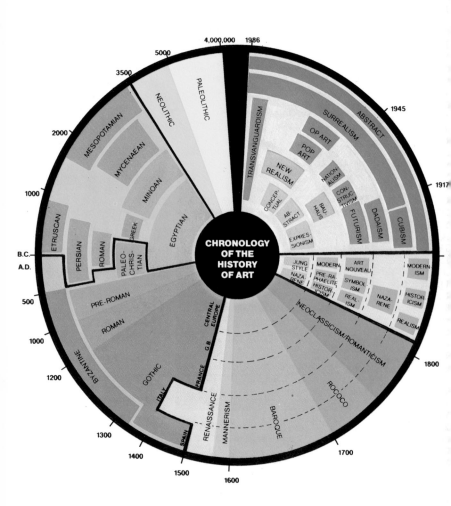

This chart shows the evolution of Western and Near Eastern art through the ages. The terms are those that art historians traditionally use to label periods of time in various cultures where definite stylistic tendencies have occurred. The books in the Key to Art series examine the interplay of artists, ideas, methods, and cultural influences that have affected the evolution of specific art styles.

INDEX OF ILLUSTRATIONS

CONTENTS

ACKNOWLEDGMENTS

Aisa: pp. 28-29, 74-75; Alte Pinakothek, Munich: p.68; A.P.: pp. 11, 24, 35, 60; Association of National Museums: pp. 3, 12, 38, 43, 55, 59, 69, 70; F. Catalá-Roca: p. 18; Fundació Miró, Barcelona: p. 76; Giraudon: p. 23, 45, 49, 56, 69; Glasgow Museum and Art Galleries, Glasgow: p. 60; I.G.D.A.: p. 53; Index: pp. 4-5, 13, 33; Kunsthistorisches Museum, Vienna: p. 58; Museum of Catalan Art, Barcelona: pp. 13, 40, 63; Museum of Modern Art, Barcelona: p. 14; National Gallery, Oslo: p. 31; The National Gallery, London: p. 19; Oronoz: pp. 26, 32, 51, 52; Picasso Museum, Barcelona: p. 36; Pollock-Krasner Foundation/ARS, N.Y.: p.27; Prado Museum, Madrid: pp. 10, 15, 30, 36, 42, 44, 57, 61, 62, 66, 67, 77; Desmond Rochfort: p. 72-73; Scala: p. 6-7, 8, 16, 17, 39, 47, 54, 64; The Tate Gallery, London: p. 70-71; Juan-Ramón Triadó: p. 20, 21.